INFATUATION:

A POEM

DELIVERED BEFORE THE

BOSTON MERCANTILE LIBRARY ASSOCIATION,

BY PARK BENJAMIN.

INFATUATION:

A POEM

SPOKEN BEFORE THE

MERCANTILE LIBRARY ASSOCIATION

OF BOSTON,

OCTOBER 9, 1844.

BY PARK BENJAMIN.

PUBLISHED BY THE ASSOCIATION.

BOSTON:
WILLIAM D. TICKNOR AND COMPANY.
MDCCCXLIV.

BOSTON:
PRINTED BY FREEMAN AND BOLLES,
WASHINGTON STREET.

INFATUATION.

Once on a time, as sacred books proclaim,
There lived a man, and Adam was his name.
Without a peer, sublimely lone, he stood
In that fair world, pronounced by Wisdom good;
Monarch of all, the last of all was he —
Lo! earth was there and firmament and sea;
Bird, beast, fish, insect, perfect in their kind,
The myriad subjects of a single mind.
Vast was his empire, uncontrolled his reign;
Lake, river, forest, mountain, desert, plain,
Wide wastes of sand beneath the torrid zone,
And isles of ice where Winter builds his throne —
All, though unseen, were his by Heaven's command,
The first great bounty of his Maker's hand.
But not the best — the best was yet to rise;
A softer star was glimmering in the skies,
A fresher flower was waiting to be born,
A sweeter warbler to salute the morn.
Thoughts, wishes, dreams, emotions, passions came,
And lit the altar of his soul with flame;

Asleep at noontide in a bower he lay,
Screened by thick foliage from the gaze of day—
Asleep indeed, if that be sleep which knows
The joy alone, the rapture of repose.
The air was hushed, and leaves no motion made
Enough to break the picture of the shade;
No note was heard, no murmur broke the spell,
And deeper slumber upon Adam fell.

He woke. What vision bright before him glowed!
Through every vein what new enchantment flowed!
What strange, sweet odors filled the purple air!
The earth how green, the firmament how fair!
How, with exulting billows, laughed the sea!
How danced the winds in sportive, tameless glee!
He knew not why, but sense and being seemed
Lost in the dawn of tender light, that beamed
Like the soft plumes of seraphs, far descried
When lovely day in lovelier evening died.
Oh, let me not with feeble pencil trace
Thy form, most beauteous of thy charming race!
Thou hadst a bard, transcendent and alone,
And now a sculptor claims thee for his own.
By Milton's muse endeared, thy beauties live
In all the fame that poetry can give;
The marble soon shall equal charms receive,
And Powers, Heaven-guided, mould a second Eve.

The happy hours, those blissful shades among,
Of our first parents minstrels oft have sung;
Bright eyes have wept and blooming cheeks grown pale,
O'er the sad pages that record the tale
Of cursed INFATUATION, which we call
With gallantry unequalled "*Adam's* fall."
Enough that he from realms of peace was hurled,
Enough that he, unhappy, lost a world;
Lost through temptation, that by woman came,
Why should the sin she prompted bear his name?
'T is ever thus: the captive hugs his chain,
The exile welcomes years of grief and pain,
The conqueror yields the empire he has won,
By woman's wiles enchanted and undone.
Yet, by parenthesis, I'm free to say
I would have been like Adam every way;
If Eve had erred, I would have shared her lot,
And ate the apple, had she asked or not:
Of her bereft, could Eden Eden prove,
Or that be Paradise which was not love?
Infatuation! in the serpent's hiss
First came thy power to banish human bliss,
To blind the spirit, dim the spark divine,
And quench the lamp that burns on Reason's shrine.
Thou wast, in oldest time, the bane, the ban,
As thou art now the plague and pest of man.

From thee spring num'rous evils, great and small,
Youth bows to thee, and manhood heeds thy call;
Maids, wives and widows hasten to obey
Thy voice, and follow where thou point'st the way:
No matter what thy words or where they lead,
Crowds rush tumultuous and fresh crowds succeed.
Thus have I seen beneath an open sky
Long lines of geese on balanced pinions fly;
Thus have I seen along a broken plain,
Full flocks of sheep run on with might and main;
Thus down the rock, that stays a river's course,
Leap the piled waters with resistless force.
Infatuation governs all by turns;
Now here, now there with various force it burns.
Fanned by the gale of popular desire,
Naught can arrest its swiftly-speeding fire,
But far and wide the flames increasing roll,
Rejoice in havoc and defy control.
So on some boundless prairie of the West,
When constant suns have scorched its fertile breast,
The hunter sees, perchance at day's decline,
When moon and stars in Heaven's soft azure shine,
Wherever he directs his wondering gaze,
The rank, tall grass for miles and miles ablaze:
Wave dashed on wave, the conflagration roars,
A sea of fire with no surrounding shores.

Secure in distance, and the gale behind,
The hunter gazes with a placid mind,
Amazed to think how one small spark, that came
From one small flint, could fill the sky with flame.
Thus, looking on with philosophic thought,
The ruin oft by human folly wrought,
The humble bard may venture to deplore
The same mad scenes enacted o'er and o'er,
And find enough, however scant and stale,
" To point a moral and adorn a tale."

Oh, Philadelphia, how dost thou disgrace
The name and creed of that peace-loving race,
That band of quiet, mild and silent men,
Who date their ancestry from William Penn !
What drops of pity must the patriot shed
When he remembers thy illustrious dead ;
When he laments thy violated trust,
Sees Riot trample on their honored dust,
And Rapine stalk with Carnage hand in hand,
Among the tombs that consecrate the land !
That land, once called the refuge of mankind,
Home of the poor and haven of the mind,
Where, free as air, th' oppressed of all the earth,
Might come like children to a father's hearth.
Tell me, my countrymen, are these the times,
Boasted in speeches, magnified in rhymes,

By turgid period and bombastic phrase
Extolled so boldly on our festal days,
When flaunting flags delight the truant eye,
And bellowing guns with loud declaimers vie?
And is this Freedom? such the welcome given,
To those who leave for our their native Heaven?
Stranger! return upon your ocean path:
Here sweeps the flood of patriotic wrath,
Here glow again the sacrilegious fires,
Here Justice droops and Charity expires.
Sometimes a convent, then a church we burn —
The pleasant pastimes that our children learn —
Anon we slay, to quell such horrid scenes —
An end that surely sanctifies the means.
Talk not of injuries: God's statutes still
From Sinai thundered, say "Thou shalt not kill."
And tell me not that all beneath our clime
Share not the blame, though guiltless of the crime.
We are Americans, by bond and blood,
From Georgia's swamps to Niagàra's flood.
Let Riot rage, or Credit sink and die,
We all are culprits in the general eye:
The voice of Europe no distinction draws,
A common country makes a common cause.
The deeds and laws of States alike unknown,
To foreign powers the Union speaks alone.

If Pennsylvania refuse to pay,
If Indiana name a distant day,
If Illinois and Mississippi act
Like brave defaulters, and confess the fact,
If Maryland suspend on either shore
Her legal payments twenty years or more —
Not they, except in name, the judgment bear,
Though on their brows the slavish brand they wear.
We are accused, *our* fame and honor lost,
And they are swindlers at the country's cost.
When will ye learn, oh ye of little faith,
That crime is worse than indigence or death?
And honesty, high theme of Franklin's pen,
Best policy of nations as of men?
Oh sage philosopher! could'st thou behold
How changed are all things since the days of old,
When from the clouds thou drew'st the lightning down,
And to poor Richard gave a wide renown;
How would amazement seize thee, at the word
Repudiation! first by mortals heard,
In this our age, our country, and confessed
The stamp, the blazon of Columbia's crest!
Unfold what counsel would be thine to-day:
What would poor Richard to his readers say?
"Oh friends! Oh brothers! hear a patriot's prayer;
Pay all your debts, no matter how or where,

Pay all your debts, leave not a penny more
Than keeps starvation from a beggar's door;
Sell your best coat, your hat, your shoes beside:
Barefooted honesty may strut in pride,
Bareheaded worth maintains a special grace,
Credit in weeds shames villainy in lace;
And he who pays is always he who rules,
For Debt makes slaves as Idleness makes fools."
Thus might the voice, which senates heard with awe,
In homely lines proclaim a righteous law.

Not bankrupt States, exulting o'er the spoil
Of riches stolen from the hoards of toil,
Not men, grown furious, as the fagot's blaze
Unveiled Christ's symbols to their fiend-like gaze;
Not these alone, with all their awful train,
Inspire deep dread and infinite disdain.
The star of empire from its westward way
On mobs and murder pours its tranquil ray.
False prophets preach and false believers throng
In fanes accursed by violence and wrong.
Still from the South, Disunion's impious hand
Flings her dark banner to the startled land,
Waves o'er the altar, which our fathers raised,
The same red torch that long in terror blazed,
Till he who ruled, a monarch save in name,
Denounced the treason and suppressed the flame.

From themes unpleasing, turn we to survey
The giddy dance that makes the people gay.
Thus after tragedy the farce appears,
And ladies smile through overflowing tears;
So smile the rainbows cloud and vapor through,
So smile the roses mid their tears of dew.
Now o'er the world Infatuation sheds
The Polka's poppies into vacant heads.
Asleep the Polka seems a tangled maze,
Awake the Polka prompts a hundred lays:
Polka the halls, the balls, the calls resound,
And Polka skims, Camilla-like, the ground.
Where roves in groves the nonsense-doating nymph,
And dreams by streams as smooth and clear as lymph,
Some leaf as brief as woman's love flits by,
And brings dear Polka to her pensive eye.
So in swift circles, backward, forward, wheeled,
The Polka's graces were at first revealed;
Perchance some posture-master, happy man,
From Nature drew the Polka's pretty plan.
Oh, wondrous figure, exquisitely stepp'd,
In thee who would not, should not be adept?
Oh Polka, Polka, wherefore art thou so?
I've asked ten dandies, and the ten "don't know!"
How wide, how absolute must be thy reign,
When ancient dames attempt the task in vain;

When modern Shatterlys affect the beau,
And feebly twirl the paralytic toe.
Oblivious, wrapped in thy delirious trance,
See girls, turned Bayadères, complete the dance,
With grace so witching and with art so true,
Ellsler might pale with envy at the view,
Cerito languish, Taglioni sigh
O'er nights of triumph passed forever by,
The modest waltz, by Byron fitly sung,
And coyly tripping from Anacreon's tongue,
Yields to the Polka's more bewildering arts,
That weave new meshes over female hearts.
We want a poet — can our clime afford
One pure as Little, moral as my lord?
Oh, spared by satire, let the passions play,
While music speaks what language cannot say!
I love to see, where Fashion holds her court,
Such harmless freedom with such pleasant sport;
It shows a proper disregard of forms,
The brain it softens and the bosom warms,
And this great truth in striking light reveals,
Where wit is absent, heads succumb to heels.

My Muse, discursive, takes a bolder spring,
And, "transcendental," soars on lofty wing.
Let none imagine that I dare to spend
My little strength upon so vast an end,

As in my language, plain as Quaker suit,
To mock the style, that strikes Creation mute.
An humbler purpose, lowlier aim be mine,
Than in fantastic, borrowed robes to shine.
Mine be the task in simple, Saxon verse,
With some faint meaning clear, direct and terse —
Though friends of cant and foes of fact despise —
An old acquaintance to apostrophize.

Hail Understanding! in the days of yore,
More prized than jewels and the golden ore;
By book-men deemed essential as the light
That guides a traveller through the gloomy night;
With Common-sense 't was thy delight to go,
Inseparably linked for weal and wo.
To faithful spouse no husband ever clung
More close than ye, ere license loosed the tongue
And taught the pen more antics to perform
Than zigzag lightnings in a summer storm.
Bound by no stronger ligament are they
Who prompted, Bulwer, thy prodigious lay!
As well might Eng from Chang attempt to fly
Or Chang to Eng forever bid good-by,
As thou, bright Understanding, to dispense
With thy twin-brother, sober Common-sense.
And are there any who have dared to part
Those joined by Nature and attached by Art?

Reply, ye mystics, minions of the moon,
Strayers in shadow while it yet is noon,
Loiterers in labyrinths without a clew,
Perverse explorers after something new;
Ye modern oracles, whose leaves contain
More hopeless riddles for the reeling brain
Than ever Sibyl, in her maddest mood,
Tossed on the wind that waved her sacred wood.
Arise, ye dim, and mutter answers odd,
Vouchsafe, like Burleigh, a mysterious nod;
Declare how sense and sound can be divorced,
How to strange jargon language can be forced,
How tropes and similes can be displayed,
Like scenes on tea-cups, landscapes on brocade,
So mixed and jumbled, twisted and turned round,
Trees elbow seas and sky contends with ground:
And how in sentences, as long as psalms,
Meaning is rare as motion is in calms.
Oh, for a blast from some rude Borean pen,
Mover of mighty, scourge of little men,
To drive afar these leaden clouds once more,
Melt the mirage, reveal the solid shore,
And over all Wit's sparkling sunshine pour.
Yet sport, ye gossamers, your little day —
Soon shall ye float like morning mist away!
From nothing nothing comes, to nothing goes;
The air's thin bubbles vanish whence they rose,

And on Fame's sea full many a gaudy sail
Buoyed by the zephyr, founders in the gale.
But let the critic, loving justice, tell
Of that respect the mystics merit well.
Wild, vain, abstruse, deluded as they are,
The cause of virtue never do they mar,
They are not scoffers, skeptics and profane,
Give law no scandal nor religion pain;
Unlike — transcendent praise! a brainless set,
Existing, scribbling, ranting, tippling yet.
Pale as their paper, poetasters ply
The furious pen and roll th' ecstatic eye,
String rhymes, regardless of rhetoric rules,
Call Dryden dull, and Pope and Cowper fools;
At one short sitting dash you off a score
Of love-lorn lyrics quicker far than Moore,
Or in a mournful, misanthropic mood,
Sing songs of shirts like any one but Hood.
Oh, silly creatures! strive to imitate
As best ye may the vices of the great,
Act noble Byron in the wild desire
To catch some spark of his immortal fire,
In vacant musing waste the hours of light,
And drink for inspiration all the night;
Not yours the triumph, but the shame and sin,
Ye lack the genius though ye have the gin!

Not such wast thou, of such the pioneer;
Oh minstrel sweet, to Hope and Memory dear!
England's best poet, Scotland's favorite son,
Thy wreath was gained before thy race was run;
While in the present thine the past appeared,
Familiar hands to thee a temple reared,
And fame and honors, that await the dead,
Laurel'd thy name and crowned thy living head.
Now thou art gone, and o'er thy sculptured tomb
Britannia bids her freshest wild-flowers bloom:
By thee her battles to the end of time
Are borne victorious in undying rhyme,
And, till her navies sink to rise no more,
Thy lyre shall sound from stormy Elsinore.
Hope has more pleasures since by thee enshrined,
And brings more solace to the troubled mind.
Oh, tender poet, let me trust and pray
That on thy soul she poured a heavenly ray;
And, never more by Time's horizon sealed,
The realms thy fancy painted, all revealed.
Thy vale, fair Wyoming, when Campbell died,
Was clothed in summer's garniture of pride;
On thy soft bosom should his rest be made,
And thou enfold him with thy deepest shade,
Where Gertrude oft by Susquehannah strayed.
Put on thy robes of sober Autumn brown
And mourn the hand that planted thy renown,

And let thy birds in saddest strains bewail
Thy poet dead — beloved, romantic vale!

Infatuation! not by them alone
Who twattle write is thy dominion shown;
For some who speak, and many more who hear,
More mad than those who write and read appear;
Those quiet keep while these go rambling round,
Peripatetics on no classic ground.
Precarious livelihoods some persons earn
By teaching folks from whom they ought to learn.
Pedlars of knowledge, far and wide they roam
To barter wares, unsaleable at home;
Such tricks of trade, such puffing and such tales,
Might vend a cargo full of damaged bales —
What waste of breath, what lavishment of sins
On one poor pack of calico and pins!
I do not marvel that to sell they try,
I only wonder that the people buy.
The partial law a license still requires
From vagrant loons whom walking never tires,
And stops the driver of a shop on wheels,
Who, uncommissioned, in bright buckets deals.
Then why, oh why should learning's pedlars be,
To vex the town, and scour the country free?

Is sense less precious grown than tin and tape?
Must hucksters qualify while dolts escape?
Forbid it, ye wise Solons of the land,
Who statutes frame that few can understand;
Who use more words to signify your will,
Than self-styled doctors when they laud a pill,
And twist up phrases into snarl and plot,
Till every sentence is a Gordian knot
Which none can loose, naught sever, but the paw
Of some great Alexander of the law.
Forbid this throng, this wandering at large,
Of private beggars at the public charge;
And make it penal for a man to prate
To crowded houses with an empty pate.
Chief, master Mesmer, for thy sleepy band,
Should whips be placed in every honest hand,
Not to chastise but quicken, lest like those
Who sink on snow, their misty brains be froze.
Such constant foldings of the hands to sleep,
But half alive these modern sluggards keep;
And, if somnambulists must ofttimes fall
When not awakened by a touch or call,
'T is passing strange that some, more stupid grown,
Permitted are to go about alone.
Great faith it needs, according to my view,
To trust in that which never could be true.

"From Nature's chain, whatever link you strike,
Tenth or ten thousandth, breaks the chain alike."
A truth immortal in immortal verse,
Which boys at school unceasingly rehearse,
But which grown men infatuated spurn,
As only fit for boys at school to learn.
Laugh not or sneer, my magnetizing friend,
I reverence things I cannot comprehend,
But doubt if Nature interrupts her rules,
To foster charlatans and tickle fools.
And yet what marvel? why the age upbraid?
Since men, like maidens, love to be betrayed,
And quacks, like rakes, though all the world detest,
Are always praised, rewarded and caressed.
Rich Vice, full-feasted, looks with scorn behind
On poor Integrity who has not dined;
Great Humbug, driving, deigns not to salute
Ignoble Science, trudging home on foot;
By Doctor Dunce is Doctor Skill reviled,
And Doctor Jackson yields to Doctor Wild.
But let the bard, who quackery makes his song,
Record this fact — her triumphs are not long;
To-day's best remedy to-morrow dreads,
And some new Mesmer turns unsteady heads.
Here one with doses infinitely small,
And there another with no dose at all;

Here one avers that naught but brandy 's sure,
And here another puffs the water cure.

Thus through all grades Infatuation sways
The minds of people in a thousand ways,
Which more white sheets would sully, fitly told,
Than the wide earth, not crammed with books, would hold.
All ages have their rages more or less,
As changeful quite as creeds or modes of dress.
From that far period of chivalric power,
When Arms and Hearts alternate ruled the hour,
When kings and princes sought the Holy Land,
And priests and hermits led a countless band;
When knights with levelled lances rode amain,
And scores of squires and serving-men were slain;
When Beauty then and then Devotion held
The world in thrall and fierce barbarians quelled;
When gay Romance the dullest brain could lure,
And every lady owned a troubadour,
Down to our day, when talents toil for pelf,
And no man fights for any but himself;
When cold Reality at Fiction mocks,
And Fancy gives no title save to stocks —
Have all mankind and mankind's better half
Bowed, like the Hebrews, to some temporal calf:
And whether low or lofty, meek or bold,
Adored that most, which most was made of gold.

Gold! matched with thee, what necromancer's arts
Can arms subdue, or conquer human hearts?
What folly, madness, could the serpent tempt,
From which thy myriad creatures are exempt?
What rage so absolute has ruled so long,
The praise of satire and the scorn of song!
More than Ambition's are thy victims told,
And Beauty bends, Devotion stoops to gold.
In the great city, full of whirl and din,
The shrine of pleasure and the haunt of sin,
Where Pity meets along the crowded way
Precocious guilt and premature decay,
And tottering eld, with looks profanely cast
On barefaced lewdness, sweeping boldly past;
Nobs with sleek steeds and snobs on meagre nags,
Pride robed in silks and Poverty in rags —
So throng the money-changers, Faith believes
That prayer's high houses are but dens of thieves.
From all Gold's votaries, let me picture one,
No object strange or new beneath the sun.
Yon pallid wretch, on whose bent brows you trace
The frequent furrows Time can ne'er efface,
Though by no hand of his implanted there,
"The slave of av'rice and low-thoughted care,"
Lives in a dungeon, drags a weary chain,
And files his mind to basest use of gain.

Wears heaven to him the aspect of a friend?
Do vernal airs one consolation lend?
Comes genial warmth in summer's early hours?
Breathes there a blessing from autumnal flowers?
Joy to his heart, and vigor to his frame,
Brings generous winter with its fireside flame?
To him alike all seasons and their change;
Few are his wishes, circumscribed their range;
Through the dull streets indifferent he goes,
When the breeze rustles, and the tempest blows.
Intent on gold, bright planets in the skies
Seem but half-eagles to his yellow eyes,
And light of poetry his soul esteems,
Except when silver mingles with its streams.
Old ere his prime, existence wastes away,
His full-fed lamp emits a flickering ray,
His once firm footsteps falter near the tomb,
Disease proclaims, and Death will seal his doom.
Some day when Fortune shall her favors send,
And brilliant luck on long-laid schemes attend,
When gained the prize for which his peace was sold,
He shall depart and leave his life in gold.

A little longer, to adorn my page,
Keep we the curtain up from Mammon's stage.
On Fancy's railroad, swift as light can range,
Adjourn with me to Gotham's vast Exchange;

Some slight amusement may the scene afford —
Who looks for wisdom at a broker's board ?
Behold a table, not with dainties spread,
But ink and pens and slender books instead.
Who are the guests ? Some fifty eager souls
Whom money charms, and lust of gain controls.
How cool and calm and yet how swift the flow
Of conversation through that ciphering row !
They question figures, figures they reply —
Those crooked falsehoods which they say can't lie.
Who would imagine thousands lost and won,
This fool enriched and that wise man undone
By words so rapid, that their sense is lost
To all save those who count and feel the cost ?
Not in your halls, Frascati, hung with lights
Enough to decorate Cimmerian nights,
Were sums more dazzling staked on red and black,
Or the weird pictures of a pasteboard pack.
There dukes with princes, lords with generals played,
Here bulls and bears promiscuous are arrayed ;
The former spent no fortunes but their own,
The latter lavish other's wealth alone.
What 's their's is no one's ; bubbles are not rocks,
The synonyme for money is not stocks ;
The high to-day, to-morrow are the low,
They come like shadows and like shadows go ;

Blown by a breath, the foam-bells upward soar,
A breath assails them and they touch the shore,
Perchance again to soar, again to sink,
And draw more venturers to Ruin's brink.
Sweet Speculation ! Circe never gave
A cup so charming as thy gilded wave :
Her's transformed men, the legend says, to swine,
But larger animals are made by thine.
And well they know who at the table sit,
Where practised cunning takes the place of wit,
Thy power to dupe, infatuate and win,
All who have what the vulgar christen "tin :"
Therefore to thee are full libations poured,
Oh fickle goddess ! at the broker's board.
Yet health to enterprise, success to trade,
Increase to wealth by honest labor made !
Long may the merchant prosper, Commerce keep
Her well-won empire o'er the subject deep.
Long through the land may Thrift by Science led,
New powers develop and new bounties spread.
Blessed be the hand, which lib'ral as the sun,
Dispenses gold by toil and talents won.
Stewards of Heaven, a few there are who live
As if to get were poorer than to give,
And more true joy in acts of kindness lay,
Than all that Fortune gives or takes away.

This truth attest, thou light that cheer'st the blind,
Attest, ye floodgates of the rayless mind,
With what a spirit Perkins can be kind:
And you, ye desolate, wherever found,
Lift your bowed brows in gladness from the ground,
And in your hymns the name of Lawrence sound!

Though, like all poets, gold I worship not,
And may not keep the little I have got,
Lest through my heart the rust of avarice eat,
And than Fame's garland money seem more sweet—
In riches fairly gained and nobly spent,
I see a longed-for prize of life, content;
Albeit the jewel we should covet most
Is Faith's and Virtue's, never Fortune's boast.
Though purse-proud cits with smoothly-shaven chins,
Who think one Sunday blots a week of sins,
And patriot sharpers, who on bargains dote,
And sell their honor as they sell their vote,
The humble man, who strives to earn his bread
The way his hands can best subserve his head,
May, with a hearty, generous hate, abjure—
He scorns to shout "the rich against the poor!"
Insensate cry! by demagogues and knaves,
Pealed in the ears of drones and dupes and slaves,

And echoed back with all a rabble's rage,
To shame republics and disgrace our age!

But cease, oh Muse! nor thus the strain prolong,
Lest it turn out a sermon, not a song;
Lest gentle sleep descend on downy plume,
And seal at once fair eyelids and my doom.
Let folly flourish! *vive la bagatelle!*
Be blithe and merry, for the world is well;
To make it better why should I aspire?
Frail is my harp and faint its master's fire;
Not his the skill to wake the slumbering mind,
Establish truth and elevate mankind.
To softer melodies that harp attune,
With sweeter visions let my thoughts commune,
And, best of all, this strain must be confessed—
The last new nonsense ever is the best.

There is a madness, gentle as the dove,
Well known to poets, and they call it *Love.*
What tales are told to celebrate its power!
What dainty ditties sung in hall and bower;
What vows! what sighs! darts, duels and despair,
Embroidered slippers, rings and locks of hair!
What tears of pleasure and what smiles of grief!
Short pain too lasting, and long joy too brief;

Though dark yet fair, a falsehood yet a truth,
Old age's retrospect and hope of youth —
Was ever so much compassed in a word,
Was ever contradiction more absurd?
By love inspired, fops take a world of pains
To prove that bodies may exist *sans* brains;
The former so fantastically dressed,
The latter's absence may be safely guessed.
By love inspired, the scholar quits his books,
And finds no learning save in Mary's looks:
How bright the lesson, how sublime the style,
Greek in her glance and Sanscrit in her smile!
By love inspired, the statesman yields the power
Of ruling senates for a lady's bower;
Great minds are swayed by passion more than fame,
Napoleon felt, and Tyler feels the flame.
By love inspired, the cautious man of trade
Starts from his store and seeks the solemn shade,
Leaves his large ledger and his "pots and pearls"
For pic-nic parties and gregarious girls.

Controlling Love! breathes there a man or boy
Who has not felt thy dear, delicious joy?
Who has not writ on paper or on slate,
Rhymes without reason, letters without date,
In praise of her, his darling that must be,
"The fair, the soft, the inexpressive she?"

If there be any, let him speak at once,
"For him have I offended!" he's a dunce,
A heartless wretch to fly thy witching toils,
And "fit for treasons, stratagems and spoils."
No music thrills his cold, insensate soul,
For him in vain the stars harmonious roll,
For him in vain the earth puts on her bloom,
The spring's gay garland decks cold winter's tomb,
The fountains flash, the frolic zephyrs play,
And budding trees assume their green array.
In vain for him, bright in her cloudless noon,
Sails the slow splendor of the harvest moon,
While the hushed landscape in the mellow beam,
Sleeps as if conscious of some happy dream.
In vain the roses, lovers of sweet dews,
For him their perfumes through the air diffuse,
And show the diamonds in their velvet laps —
At him in vain the ladies set their caps.
He lives that lonely, miserable thing,
Of whom, to frighten babies, nurses sing;
A horrid, hateful, selfish, naughty one,
Whom matrons scandalize and misses shun,
Whom no brief nights console for tedious days,
Yclept a bachelor, in common phrase;
Yet would I not with recreant jest profane,
Controlling Love, thy undisputed reign.

What though to me thou hast no favor shown,
I kneel, still suppliant, at thy air-built throne;
Thy smile's sweet promise single men resign,
But when life's ray itself has ceased to shine.
Oh charming folly, beautiful deceit,
Making rough smooth, dim clear, and bitter sweet,
If thou'rt a phantom, still let me pursue,
A fond delusion, still believe thee true!

A word to close this free discursive strain —
Not uttered idly, nor I trust in vain.
Your summons hither promptly I obeyed,
A little frightened, though not quite dismayed:
What! write a poem in these railroad times?
Supply young merchants with domestic rhymes,
Not for protection or revenue named,
In the "black tariff" so unwisely framed
That wealth rewards the sturdy lab'rer's hand,
And blooming plenty blesses all the land?
A home-made poem! made to order, too,
And for Bostonians — ah! what can I do?
Boston — the mart of literature and taste,
Where diamonds pass for diamonds, paste is paste!
Have they no bards, no minstrels of their own?
Has Sprague's high muse to ampler regions flown?
Is the pure lyre of Dana silent still?
Flows not "Hyperion" at his own sweet will?

Where murmurs now the harp of Palestine?
And where that gay, enchanting verse of thine,
My early friend, whose faintest numbers fell
Like the clear cadence of a deep-toned bell?
Still, slave and conqueror of science, roams
Where duty bids, the brilliant mind of Holmes.
Hard is the task to sing, when music fails
In such a nest of tuneful nightingales.
I thought of Lessing's fable, and applied
Its humbling moral to my soaring pride.
Let me not try too bold, too grand a strain,
Plain is my subject, let my verse be plain.
Resolving thus, my rapid pen sped o'er,
Like some light bark that seeks a grateful shore,
A sea of paper — has it sought in vain
Attendant friends, that grateful shore to gain?
Has my swift voyage a single care beguiled?
On my recital has one kind lip smiled?
If any so *infatuated* be,
Right welcome is such guerdon unto me.
For such, what songster would not dare to try
His feeble plumes beneath a fav'ring sky?

Yet let me not deny a loftier aim
Than that which I have ventured thus to claim.
If by my aid one truth has triumphed, then
Contented I resign thee, faithful pen!

Go to thy rest, where never hand of mine,
Can trace with thee the rude, yet earnest line;
Go to thy rest with all that thou hast done—
Sallies of sense, experiments at fun,
Songs, sonnets, satires, epigrams and plays,
The sport of younger, toil of older days;
Let none survive, (a most superfluous prayer,)
But all thy quiet, thy oblivion share!
Then unregardful of your praise or blame,
Ye critic-tribe, ye almoners of fame!
I shall beg nothing of your mercy, save
A name unnoted and a peaceful grave.
Enough for me, if partial love can tell
'He worshipped *truth*, and kept her precepts well,
'The false he hated, though the world received,
'And in imposture never once believed,
'He loved his kind, but sought the love of few,
'And valued old opinions more than new.'
Be this my epitaph: from man I ask,
This meed alone for Life's laborious task;
No further recompense, no more renown,
No greener laurel and no brighter crown.

www.ingramcontent.com/pod-product-compliance
Lightning Source LLC
LaVergne TN
LVHW011125110826
845150LV00008B/2254

* 9 7 8 1 4 1 8 1 9 4 7 7 2 *